Needle Crafts 19
MACHINE PATCHWORK

SEARCH PRESS
Tunbridge Wells

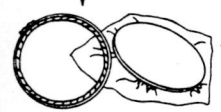
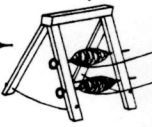

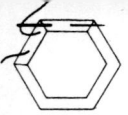

INTRODUCTION

Patchwork is a satisfying and creative craft. Originally the patches were sewn by hand but, with modern machines, patchwork can be made quickly, with stronger stitching, and a wider range of fabrics can be used. Most of the equipment needed for machine patchwork will already be available in the home, and the craft needs no specialised design knowledge. This book deals with the repeated block designs but the techniques described can be adapted to suit any pattern. Patterns are open to individual choice of colour and fabric, and no two will look alike even if the same block is used.

EQUIPMENT

Since patchwork requires very accurate measuring and cutting, the best results will be achieved if you invest in a few basic tools.

For designing and making templates

Coloured pencils and felt tip pens; square and triangular graph paper; metal ruler; 2H lead pencil; scissors (for cutting paper); scalpel knife with replaceable blades; spray adhesive; heavyweight card; set-square (all obtainable from art suppliers).

For stitching

A sewing machine that makes a good even running-stitch, and preferably a reverse stitch: a steam iron and pressing cloth; needles; cotton-polyester thread, lace pins; seam ripper; dress-makers scissors, small scissors (for cutting ends); tape measure.

For quilting

Quilting hoop; needles (between 8–9), thimble; quilting thread, beeswax; ordinary coloured pencil; rug needle.

FABRICS

It is important that fabrics to be used for patchwork are chosen with consideration for the project and its use, type of design and washability. Many traditional quilts have not survived because they were made from used clothing and filled with a well-worn blanket.

Top fabric

Cotton dress weight fabrics are the easiest to use. They are very hard-wearing and give excellent results. They press well and are suitable for all shapes. It is important, if the patchwork is to be washed, that the fabrics are pre-shrunk and fast dyed. (Batiks and Indian cotton fabrics do not seem to retain the dye well.) Today cotton fabrics are often replaced with cotton/polyester mixtures which tend to be springy and crease resistant. These are much easier to sew by machine than by hand. When they are mixed with cotton fabrics, however, take special care with the ironing of the completed patchwork — polyesters require a much lower ironing temperature.

The strength of machine sewing enables a great range of fabrics to be considered for making patchwork. Tweeds, suitings, corduroys, denim and gaberdine all have interesting textures and, providing the patches are fairly large and simple, can be used successfully for warm bed quilts, curtains and floor coverings.

Silks, satins, brocades and velvets are the most difficult to sew and handle. They are more suitable for wall-hangings and decorative uses which require little cleaning.

Do not mix fabrics of varying weights within a patchwork project as the heavier ones tend to pull and tear the lighter patches. Avoid stretchy fabrics that do not retain the correct size and shape. Choose a soft fabric if the patchwork is to be hand-quilted.

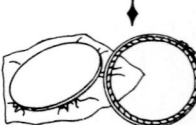

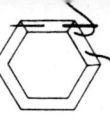

Wadding or filling

If you intend to quilt your patchwork a wadding or filling is sandwiched between the top and the backing. There are a variety available — the washable, synthetic Terylene and Courtelle waddings are very popular, light-weight and easy to use. They come in different weights: the 60g (2oz) is the thinnest and easiest for both hand- and machine-quilting, the bouncy 125g (4oz) and 250g (8oz) weights are best for knotting (or tufting). Cotton wadding, woollen and cotton domettes are heavier than the synthetic waddings but less bulky. They add weight to a quilt but create a flatter effect. They are excellent for machine quilting.

Backing fabric

Cheaper dress weight cottons are suitable for most patchwork backing.

Whether a patchwork is going to be hand-quilted or not affects the choice of fabrics. For hand-quilting choose a backing fabric that is soft and easy to pierce with a needle. Sheeting, although the size is ideal, is often so closely woven that quilting is made difficult.

BLOCK PATTERNS

The early American quilt-makers developed the block patterns, which used up scraps of fabric and enabled a large patchwork to be made relatively easily in cramped living conditions. They developed the patterns by folding squares of paper, then cutting out the shapes and using these for templates. A single-block pattern is usually square and made up of geometric shapes.

When a number of blocks are set (joined) together a variety of patterns is made. The simple shapes and straight seams make them ideal for machine patchwork. Block patterns can usually be divided into basic categories based on the number of squares into which a block can be divided.

Number of squares

It is useful for the quilt-maker to recognise these categories for construction is then easier to understand.

The four-patch is the simplest. The block is divided into four equal squares — and includes blocks with multiples of four, sixteen and sixty-four squares.

The nine-patch is the best known, and also includes blocks divided into thirty-six squares.

The five-patch is divided into twenty-five squares, and the seven-patch has forty-nine squares.

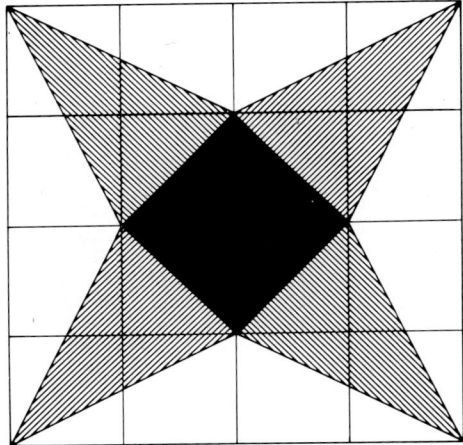

Fig. 1. A simple four-patch block, containing 16 squares.

Front cover (detail) and page 4:
'Hotpotch' quilt. *'Churn Dash' block. Made from sentimental scraps of cotton, backed with an old flannelette sheet, with a separate bound edge. Machine-pieced. The hand-quilting is minimal to allow the fabric pattern full emphasis. (Phyllis Harris)*

Page 5:
Medallion wall hanging. *'Goose Wing' design on the outer border. Machine-pieced and hand-quilted, made of pure cotton scraps. (Ann Ohlenschlager)*

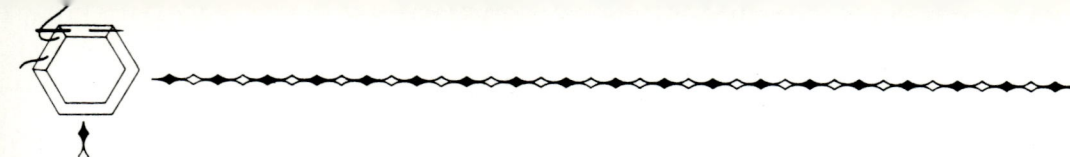

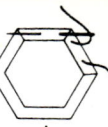

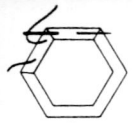

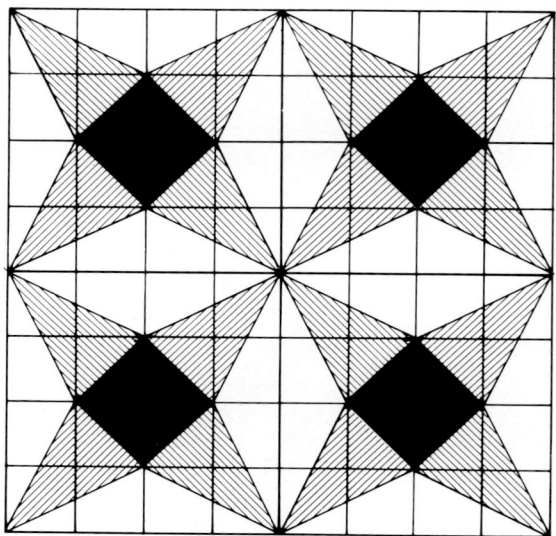

Fig. 2. Four blocks set together. Notice a new pattern appearing in the centre.

Design

Planning your patchwork is very important. This means working out the size, pattern, colours and finally, fabrics.

One way of designing is to work on graph paper with coloured pens or pencils using a one-centimetre square for each square in a block. Choose a block you like, then set four together and colour in the shapes. The blocks can also be set diagonally but extra half-blocks are needed to fill in the edges. Some people find designing with coloured pencils difficult to relate to the final choice of fabrics. An alternative method, therefore, is to cut out 25–30mm (1in.) squares of fabric and stick these on the graph paper. This allows greater flexibility in designing, although the fabric patterns will not be to the scale of the final patch size.

Size (see also note on page 31)

When choosing a block pattern make sure that it is suitable for the size of the project, for in machine patchwork the patches themselves should not be too small and fiddly to sew. Start with a simple block pattern, such as Bow-ties, which can be made up into a cushion.

A cot quilt could be a simple four-patch block repeated, such as the Windmill block, each one about 20cm (8in.) square (see fig. 4). You will need about 20 blocks, four across and five down. Most blocks on full-size patchwork quilts measure about 30 cm (12in.) square. If you are designing a bed quilt it is a good idea to make enough blocks to cover the top of the bed, then use a plain border to hang over the sides, and finish with a narrow patchwork strip around the edges. Plain or patchwork borders are useful for making the project up to the required size and help to frame the design. Another way of increasing the area of your patchwork without making more blocks is to set the blocks with lattice strips. These frame the individual blocks and are also a useful way of harmonising a scrap quilt. Alternating pieced blocks with plain squares is yet another method.

Make a design to scale

Whatever pattern you choose, make a design to scale on graph paper which shows the size of each patch, the number of blocks, borders, and colours (as in fig. 4). From this you can estimate templates and fabrics and use it as a guide to making up the patchwork. It is important to work out your project thoroughly before embarking on cutting fabrics and sewing, and the extra time spent in such planning will make the following stages easier and quicker to accomplish.

TEMPLATES

Templates are made when the design and the size has been decided. A template is needed for each individual shape within a design. They must be very accurate because they are the shapes from which the fabric patches are cut, and if they are only slightly incorrect

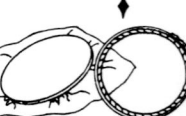

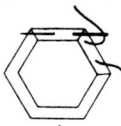

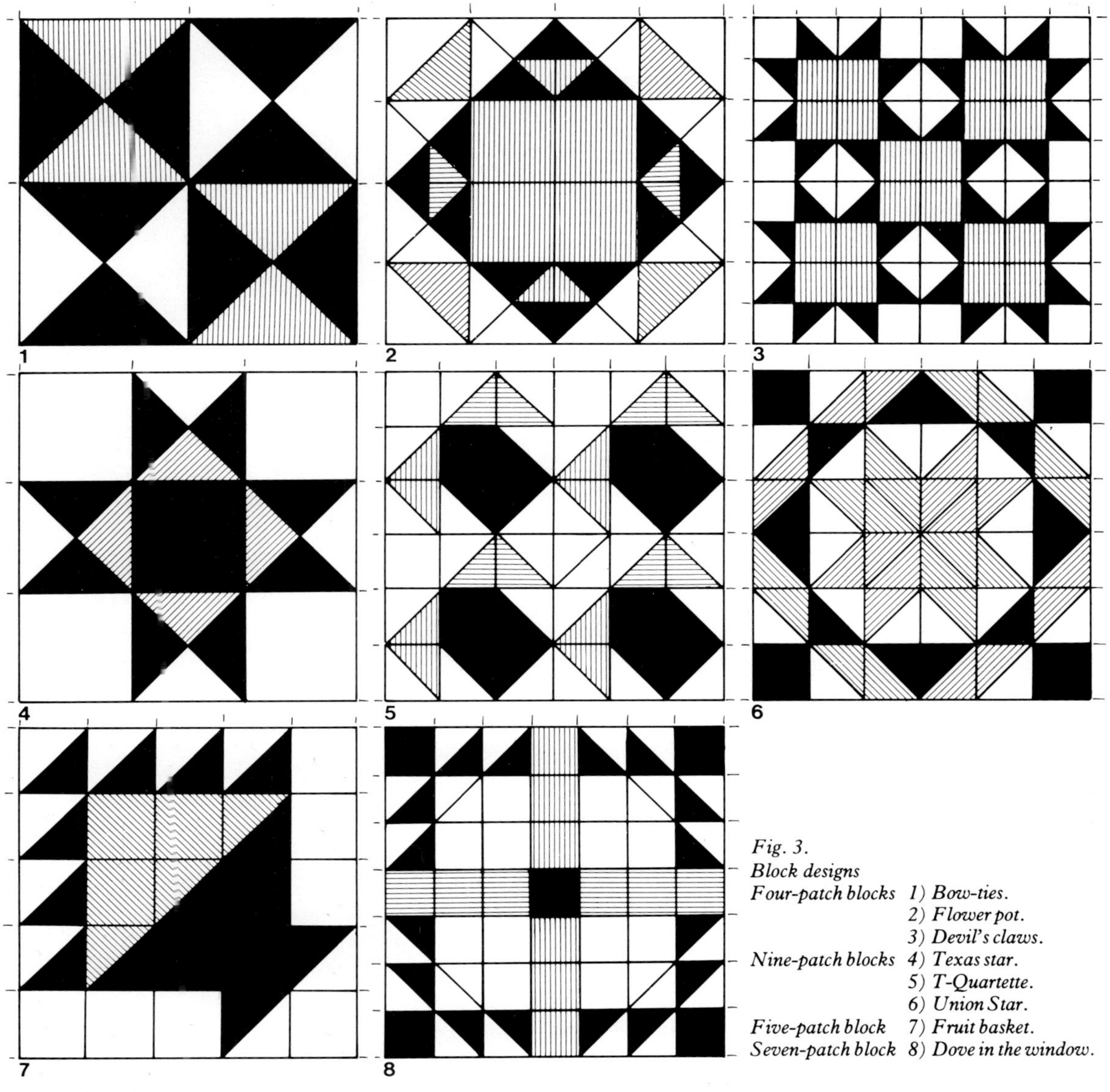

Fig. 3.
Block designs

Four-patch blocks 1) *Bow-ties.*
                        2) *Flower pot.*
                        3) *Devil's claws.*
Nine-patch blocks 4) *Texas star.*
                        5) *T-Quartette.*
                        6) *Union Star.*
Five-patch block 7) *Fruit basket.*
Seven-patch block 8) *Dove in the window.*

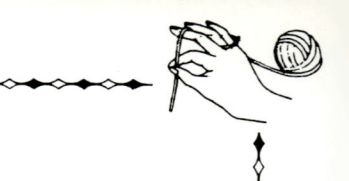

this will accumulate over a number of patches. Templates for machine patchwork must include the size of the finished patch and 6mm (¼in.) seam allowance on all edges. (This seam allowance is predetermined by the presser foot; see page 14.) To guarantee accuracy, draw out the block to be used on graph paper, using a metal ruler and a well-sharpened 2H pencil. Carefully cut out the different shapes that are needed, using the metal ruler and a scalpel knife. Stick them on thick card or sandpaper — sandpaper does not wear so well but it adheres to the fabric better than card — then add 6mm (¼in.) seam allowance on all sides and cut out (fig. 5a and 5b). Window templates are useful in framing a particular area of fabric to be used. Make them in the usual way, but cut out the centre around the edge of the finished size (fig. 5d).

Fig. 4. A scale drawing showing a repeated Windmill block design used for a cot quilt.

Page 8:
Cushion. 'Blazing Star' block, in cottons. Machine pieced. Hand quilted in a pattern that echoes the fabric design. (Anne Sellars)

Page 9:
Cushion. 'Variable Star' block. Machine-pieced and hand-quilted. Made of curtain scraps. (Doreen Harding)

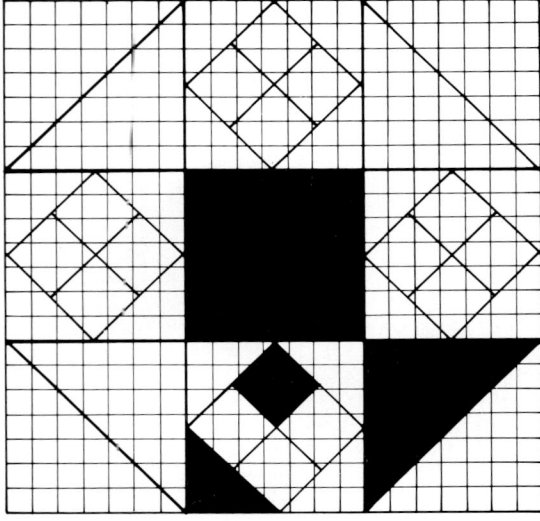

Fig. 5a. Draw out the block to the finished size (without seam allowances).

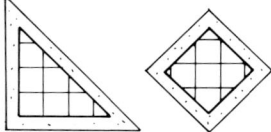

Fig. 5b. Glue shapes to card or sandpaper, add 6mm (¼in.) seam all round.

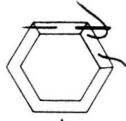

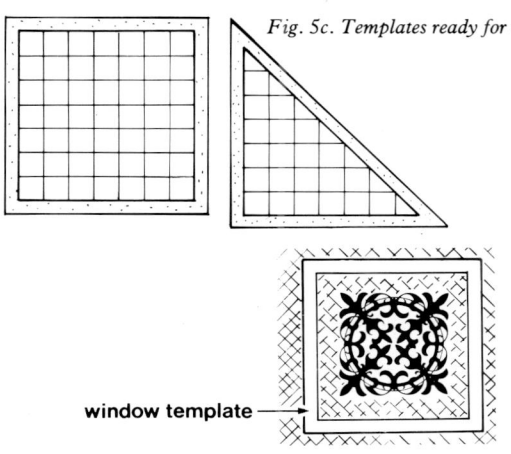

Fig. 5c. Templates ready for use.

Fig. 5d. Window template centred on motif. The inner edge is the sewing line, and the outer edge is the fabric cutting line.

CHOOSING FABRIC PATTERNS

Using fabrics together successfully is often more difficult than acquiring the techniques of sewing patchwork together. Combining different patterned fabrics comes with practice, but patchwork designs need contrasts to be effective. A variety of shapes, lights and darks and different scales of pattern will give a more exciting design than a collection of small-scale prints that eliminate the individual shapes and produce a generally bland effect. Have a variety of fabrics in prints and plain colours, combine small, medium and large-scale prints together, and use border patterns to frame a design. Curved patterns often create a sense of movement, while stripes give direction to a design — they are also good for lattice strips.

CHOOSING COLOURS

Colours change next to each other, and what may appear to be a dark patch often seems much lighter beside another fabric.

Generally bright and light colours stand out, while dark and dull colours recede; but if you are not sure of the tonal values look at them with your eyes half-closed to eliminate the pattern.

A scrap quilt is often the most difficult to plan because of the variety of prints. It is then useful either to sort the fabrics into lights and darks, or to supplement them with a quantity of fabric in a single colour. Buying bags of scraps (providing they are good value) or exchanging fabrics with friends can introduce fresh colours and patterns that you may not have considered choosing for yourself. Try and build up your own collection of fabrics, buy them when you see something interesting or suitable for patchwork. Colours are much influenced by fashion and are often available for only one season.

ESTIMATING FABRICS

It is important to be able to estimate accurately the amount of fabric required, and this can only be done when the templates have been made and the number of patches calculated. Always include seam allowances (*see over*). Estimating fabric depends on how many times a template can be laid across a width of fabric, selvedge to selvedge. Always place as many edges of the template as possible either on the straight grain which runs parallel to the selvedge, or on the cross-grain. Avoid the bias (which has the most stretch) as much as possible. Divide the total number of patches by the number fitted across a width of fabric, then multiply that number by the width of the template. Butt the templates together leaving no space in between. Estimate in this way for each different template and type of fabric used. Also, use the width of fabric as a guideline for estimating borders and lattice strips. It is wise to add 25cm (10in.) extra for safety.

Page 12:
Bordered mat. 'Variable Star' block. Machine-pieced. Machine-quilted. Log Cabin patchwork border. (Mary Thomson)
Page 13:
Shoulder bag. 'Variable Star' block. Machine-pieced and hand-quilted. Made in calico, some pieces knitted in calico strips — the handle and gusset were knitted in one continuous strip. (Pamela Watts)

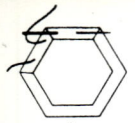

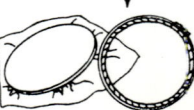

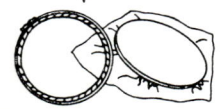

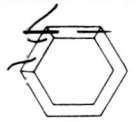

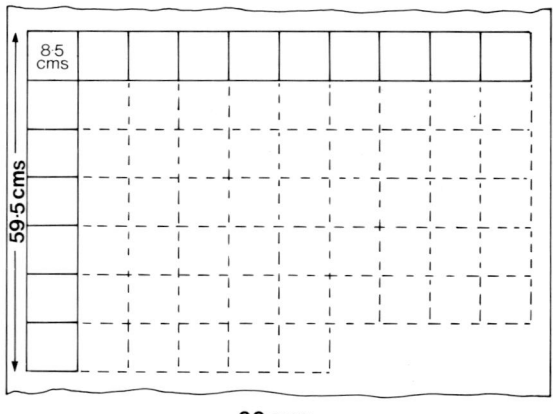

Fig. 6. Cutting layout. To cut out 66 squares each measuring 8.5cm (3³/₅in.) you would need 59.5cm (23³/₅in.) of 90cm (36in.) wide fabric.

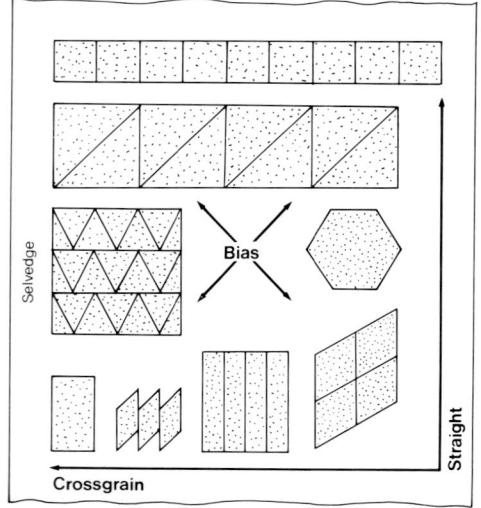

Fig. 7. As many sides of a template as possible should be on the straight or cross-grain of the fabric.

MARKING AND CUTTING FABRICS

Always wash the fabrics, if necessary, and iron them flat before use. Mark the fabrics on the reverse side with a well-sharpened coloured pencil. Never use biros or felt tip pens which will stain the fabric and templates. To stop the fabric from slipping, lay it over an old sheet or suchlike. Try and match the fabric grain to the edges of the template. Mark around each template carefully, for machine patchwork depends on accurate marking and cutting. No seam-lines are drawn. Avoid the selvedges which are often marked and uneven. Cut each patch out separately. Fabric used for borders can be torn *if the grain is straight*, but check this before you tear any large amounts.

PREPARATION FOR SEWING

When all the patches have been cut, lay out the design. Although it will not fit together very well, it enables you to check for design mistakes which are easier to rectify at this stage.

Seam allowance

Machine patchwork depends on lining up the edge of the patches with the outer edge of the presser foot. On most machines this gives a 6mm (¼in.) seam allowance. If it does not, mark the measurement on the plate with masking tape and align the fabric against the edge. Keep a constant seam allowance throughout the project, otherwise the patches will not fit together accurately.

Sewing

Tacking is unnecessary. Pin the patches right sides together, keeping the pins horizontal to the edge being sewn. Set the machine to about five stitches per 1cm (⅖in.), and use a neutral-colour thread. Feed the patches carefully through the machine, removing the pins before they go under the pressure foot. Begin and end with a couple of back stitches to prevent the ends unravelling.

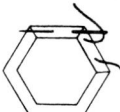

Pressing

Always press connecting seams open before joining the next patch. Because machine stitches are much stronger than those sewn by hand, press all the seams open throughout the patchwork in order to reduce bulk and make it easier to match aligning seams. Press first on the back, then on the front, using a pressing cloth to prevent glazing.

Construction

Join the smallest units together first, then join them into rows and finally sew the rows together. Pin both sides of matching seams to keep them in position, and ease in any fullness with pins. A large quilt could be completed in thirds, which are then joined.

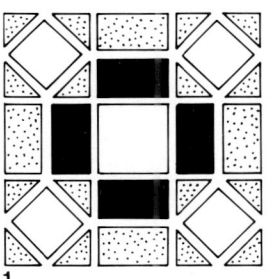
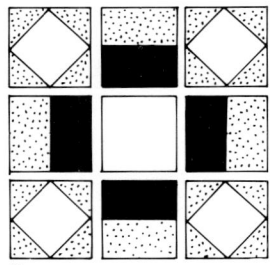

1　　　　　　　　2

Fig. 8a. Pieces of a block laid out in correct positions.　　*Fig. 8b. Squares assembled.*

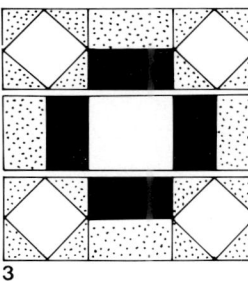
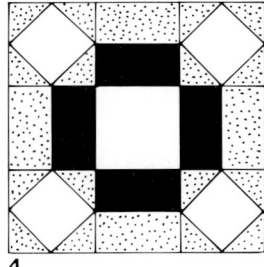

3　　　　　　　　4

Fig. 8c. Squares sewn together in rows.　　*Fig. 8d. Rows joined.*

LATTICE STRIPS

Using lattice strips is a good way of making up a patchwork quickly with fewer blocks.

They are added when the blocks are completed. One set of strips should be cut to the height of a block (including seam allowances) and a second set should measure the width of a row (which includes the blocks and strips sewn together). Sew all the blocks together into rows, alternating blocks and strips of lattice. Then join the rows together with the long lattice strips between each.

Fig. 9. Lattice strips.

Page 16:
Cushion. *'Martha Washington Star' block, with Seminole patchwork border. Machine-pieced and hand-quilted. Made in shot silk, with polyester wadding. (Pamela Watts)*
Page 17:
Class quilt, *made by a group. 'Sherman's March' block. Machine-pieced and hand-quilted in circle pattern. (Owned by Ruth Facey)*

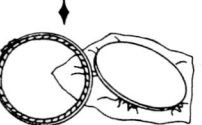

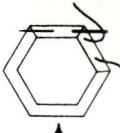

BORDERS

A border should be considered part of the original design. It can consist of plain strips or of patchwork. A border looks neater if the seams within it align with those in the main patchwork. This is particularly important when several lengths of plain fabric are joined together. If a patchwork border is used it needs to flow evenly around the main design since patches should not be cut to odd shapes in order to fit in. Turning corners is particularly difficult. It is often easier to consider these as separate squares.

Making up borders

Patchwork may not keep exactly to the original size, for fabrics often stretch, especially around the edges. It is important when making up borders, however, to refer back to the original design for the sizes, and to make the patchwork fit either by easing in fullness or slightly stretching. This ensures that the borders lie flat and the overall size is not uneven. Borders can be attached in several ways. The simplest method is to make two strips corresponding to the length of the patchwork. (Remember to include seam allowances in all measurements.) Join these to the sides, using the same sewing method as the main patchwork. Then cut two strips corresponding to the width of the patchwork plus the width of the strips on each side; join these to the top and bottom. Press all seams open.

Fig. 10. The Wild Goose Chase border is an example of one that can change directions at the corner and centre.

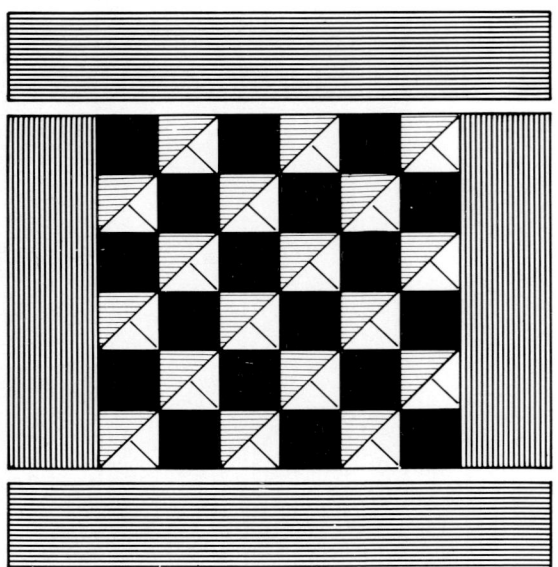

Fig. 11. Simple straight-cut borders are the easiest way to frame a patchwork.

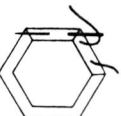

Separate corner squares

Another method is to make the borders with separate corner squares. Four strips are made to correspond to the sides of the patchwork, and four squares to correspond to the width of the strips. The strips are joined in the same order as the previous method, but the top and bottom strips include a square at each end.

Mitred corners

Mitred corners are an elegant way to complete a plain border, or they can be used on bias strips or self-binding edges (see page 30). Make two strips the length of the patchwork plus two widths of the strip, and two further strips the width of the patchwork plus two widths of the strip.

Attach them in the usual way, first to the sides, then to the top and bottom, letting the ends extend to the corners. On the top and bottom strips in each of the four corners make a diagonal fold from the inside to the outer corner. Press the fabric under and hand-sew to the strip beneath.

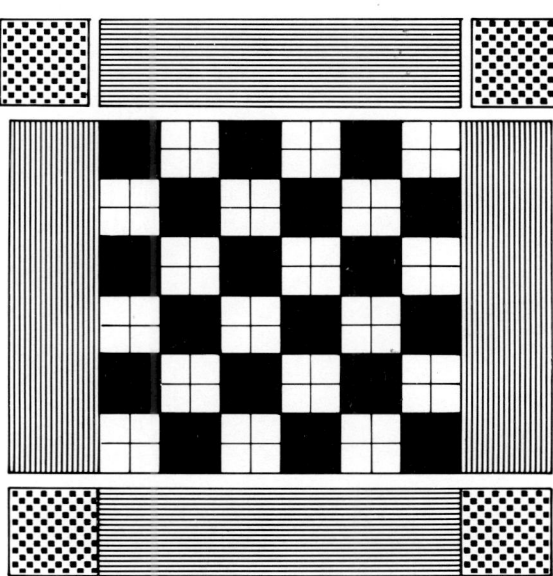

Fig. 12. Contrasting squares add interest to the corners.

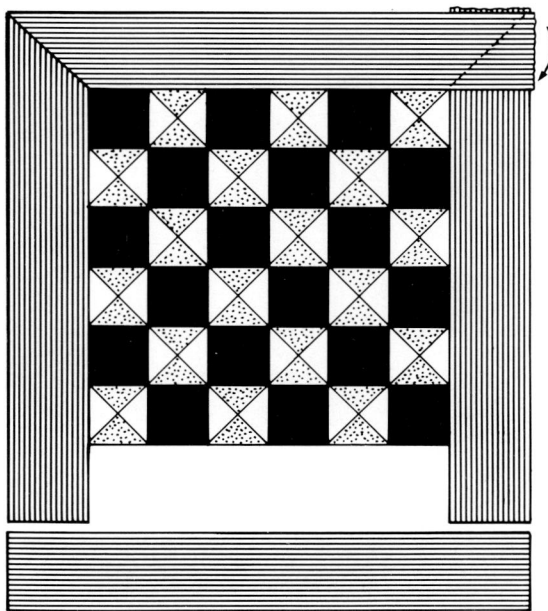

Fig. 13. Mitred corners are a simple but effective method of completing a plain border.

Page 20 and 21:
Pair of cushions *made of scraps. 'Grandmothers' Fan' and 'Variable Star' blocks. Machine-pieced and hand-quilted. Finished with plain piping. Pure cotton. (June Bowles)*

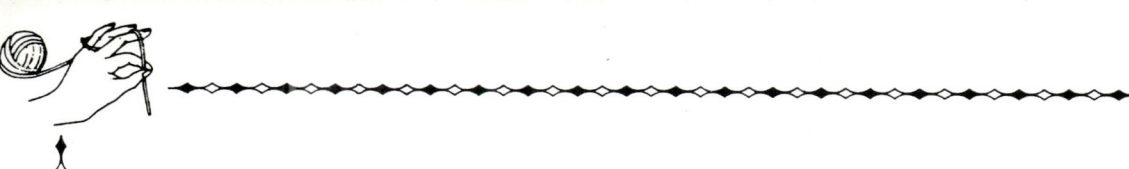

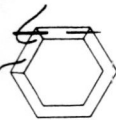

BACKING (OR LINING)

If a patchwork is not quilted it needs to be backed, as this will conceal the raw edges, give body to the work and strengthen it (it is unnecessary to line patchwork intended for cushions). Cut a piece of backing the same size as the top, but including the seam allowances. Place the right sides together and smooth them flat. Pin, then tack around the three edges, and sew together. Turn to the right side and hem-stitch the remaining edge by hand. For extra weight and warmth a sheet of cotton domette (similar to flannelette) can be used as a filling. Knot the three layers together as described on page 30.

QUILTING

Quilting gives extra warmth and decoration to the patchwork and is the sewing together of three layers — the top, the filling or wadding, and a backing fabric.

There are no design rules for quilting patchwork. Contour quilting is popular and follows the shape of the patches about 4mm (⅙in.) from the seam lines. Quilting generally gives a more interesting texture to the surface and should add to the overall effect and be considered at the design stage with the patchwork.

Marking the fabric

If the quilting design needs to be marked on the patchwork it is much easier to do this before the three layers are tacked together. Work out your pattern on the original patchwork design to ensure that it fits.

Commercial stencils can be used, or the pattern can be marked out using a metre rule. Masking tape also makes a quick and effective guideline and, provided the design is worked out beforehand, can be applied when the work is in the hoop. Use a well-sharpened coloured pencil for marking the patchwork. Traditionally, quilting lines are often marked with a rug needle, held and pressed down firmly almost parallel to the work. It works best on a padded surface and leaves an indented line marking out the pattern. Fold the fabric in quarters and mark the centre lines by pressing.

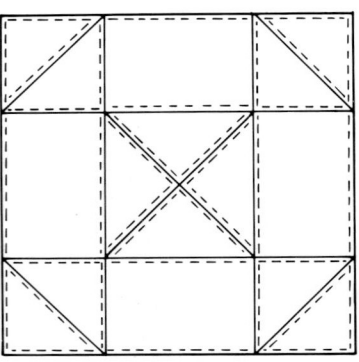

Fig. 14a. Contour quilting.

Fig. 14b/c. Contour quilting on curved seams.

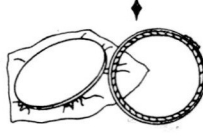

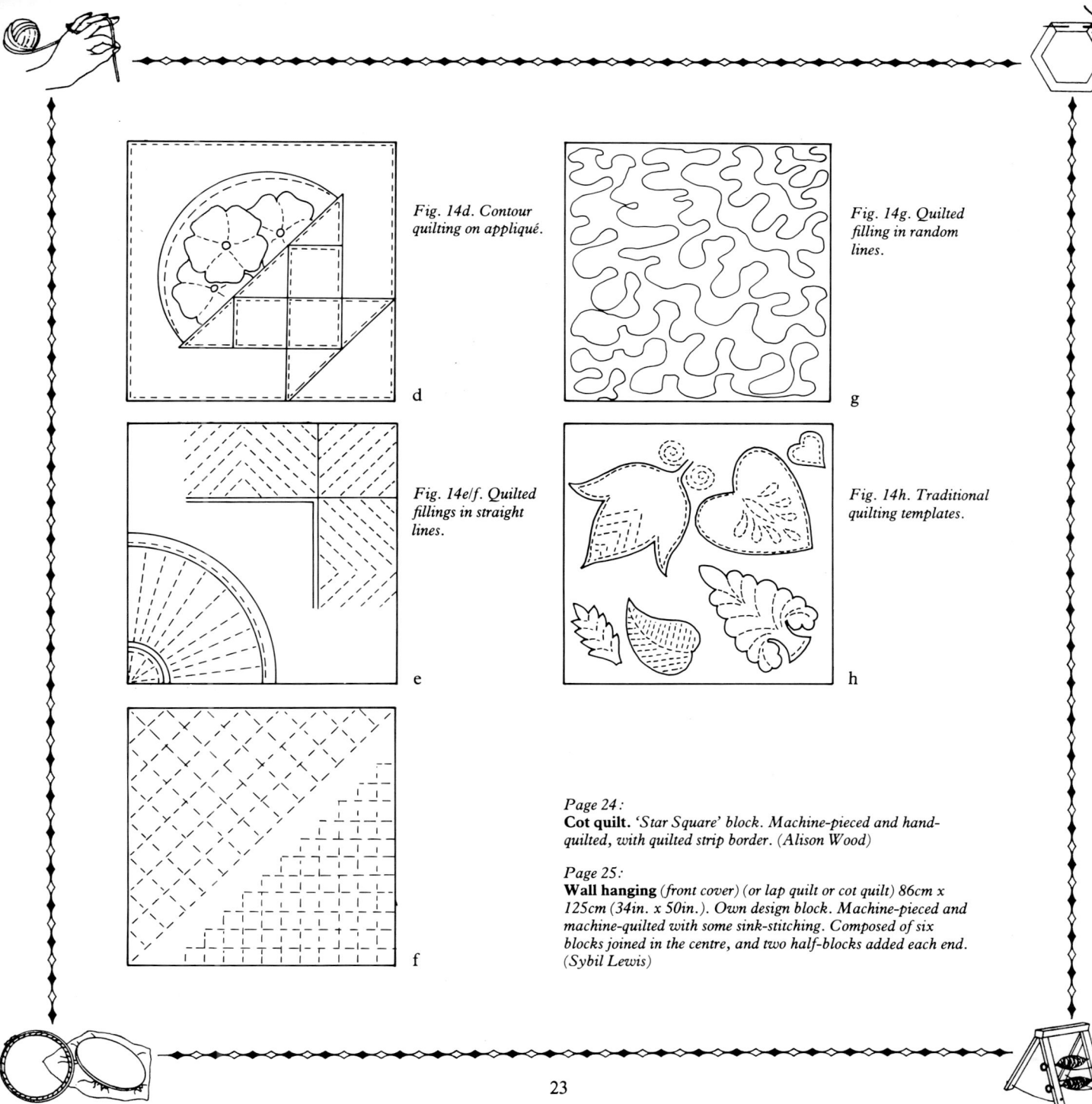

Fig. 14d. Contour quilting on appliqué.

Fig. 14e/f. Quilted fillings in straight lines.

Fig. 14g. Quilted filling in random lines.

Fig. 14h. Traditional quilting templates.

Page 24:
Cot quilt. *'Star Square' block. Machine-pieced and hand-quilted, with quilted strip border. (Alison Wood)*

Page 25:
Wall hanging *(front cover) (or lap quilt or cot quilt) 86cm x 125cm (34in. x 50in.). Own design block. Machine-pieced and machine-quilted with some sink-stitching. Composed of six blocks joined in the centre, and two half-blocks added each end. (Sybil Lewis)*

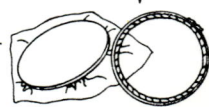

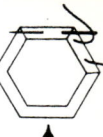

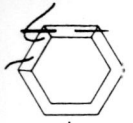

Assembly and tacking

Cut the wadding and backing fabric about 10cm (4in.) bigger on all sides than the patchwork. This allows for shrinkage due to quilting and provides a self-binding if required.

Whether you quilt by hand or machine, it is important to tack the layers thoroughly together. Lay the backing fabric on a flat surface, wrong side up, and stick the corners flat with masking tape. Lay the wadding on top, smooth it flat, then spread over the patchwork, right side up. Pin the three layers together, then tack, always working from the centre outwards to ease out any excess fabric. Cover the area thoroughly with an even distribution of tacking lines.

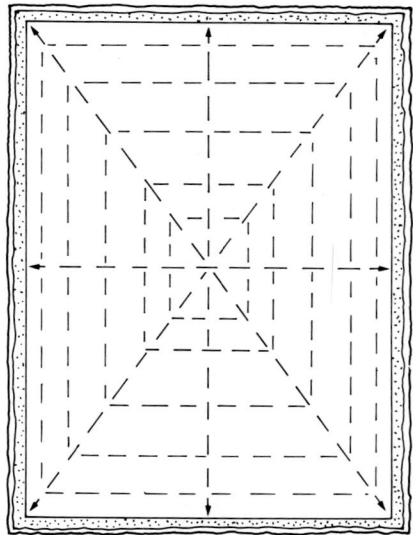

Fig. 15. The three layers tacked ready for quilting.

HAND QUILTING

Use a hoop

Unless you are quilting a small item it is better to use either a frame or a hoop. A large quilt hoop is more manageable than a frame and just as effective. It is very important to keep the three layers evenly stretched, so when setting up make sure that the backing is smooth and flat. Rest the top of the hoop on the edge of a table so that both hands can be free to work.

Thread

Use a strong single-twisted cotton thread which is especially manufactured for quilting. Match the colour to the background, or use the same neutral colour all over.

Quilting stitch

The quilting stitch is a small running-stitch, evenly spaced; it should look identical back and front. The stitches are much less obvious on patterned fabric. Always use a fairly short length of thread (about 40cm or 16in). and run it through beeswax. Knot the end you cut, to prevent twisting. To start, thread the needle and come up through the back, and pull the knot through the backing fabric so that it is held beneath the wadding. Push the needle through from the top with a thimble worn on the middle finger of the sewing hand, and keep the other hand beneath the work so that when the needle comes through it can be guided back up again. Make sure that each stitch goes through all the layers. On the sewing hand keep the thumb pressed down on the fabric just ahead of the stitching. Keep the layers of fabric in the hoop a little slack, so that eventually you can take up several stitches at once.

To finish off, tie a knot in the thread close to the last stitch, take the thread through to the back and give a quick tug to pull the knot into the wadding. Bring the thread up to the top and cut close.

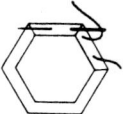

MACHINE QUILTING

Work to be quilted by machine needs to be tacked just as thoroughly as that prepared for hand quilting. Set the regulator for a slightly longer stitch than for general sewing. Use a cotton polyester thread. Machine-quilting is quicker than hand-quilting, but it is not an easier alternative. The quilting has a harder line, while the effect is much flatter and less sympathetic to traditional patchwork. For this reason machine-quilting is sometimes better if hidden in the seams — this produces a mirror image on the back and is known as 'sink stitching'. When working this, press the fabric well and open the seam as much as possible to allow the needle to pass through the centre.

Wadding

Thinner wadding is required for machine-quilting, which is not suited to the springy synthetic types. Use cotton or woollen domette or cotton wadding. These all give more weight and a less raised surface which is an advantage for wall-hangings and bed quilts. The disadvantage is that the patchwork will have to be dry-cleaned.

Stitching

It is important when machine-quilting that the layers can be fed easily under the machine foot. Alternate the beginning and end of a quilted line of stitches on each row. Do not finish off with back stitches; take the ends through to the back and fasten them off by hand.

Assembly

Start with a fairly small project, for it requires experience to manage large areas of quilted fabric.

It is easier to quilt a large item in quarters or sections and then sew these together. Patchwork blocks can be quilted individually and then joined together in rows in the usual way. If you use this method it is important to allow a little extra wadding and backing, and then trim them to size. To ensure that the blocks are all the same size before joining them, make a large template the finished size of the block plus a 6mm (¼in.) seam allowance on all sides, and trim the blocks to this. When they are joined, trim off the excess wadding in the seam allowances at the back, and lightly press the seams open. At the back, these can be covered with hand-stitched seam binding, or covered all over with a separate backing.

Pressing

If the filling is cotton or woollen domette, flannelette or cotton wadding, the patchwork can be pressed lightly with a warm iron. If any of the patchwork contains polyester fibres, remember that these need a lower heat than cotton.

Synthetic waddings cannot be ironed without losing most of their thickness.

Page 28:
Throw quilt. *'Double Irish Chain' block, machine-pieced and hand-quilted, with some hand-appliqué. Cotton and polyester cotton with terylene batting. Two separate ten-inch blocks were set next to each other. The squares in one block are machine-pieced, and four corner squares in the next block are hand-applied on to a plain white square. (Alison Martin)*

Page 29:
Place mat. *'Card Trick' block. Machine-pieced and hand-quilted. Borders in Seminole strip patchwork. (Pamela Greaves)*

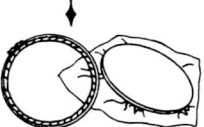

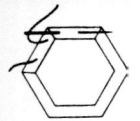

KNOTTING OR TUFTING

Where any wadding is used, the three layers must be kept securely together. Knotting (or tufting) is a quick and effective alternative to quilting.

Use a non-synthetic thick thread that will hold a knot. Heavy crochet cotton is ideal. Do not use wool because it becomes matted with use.

Make a reef knot through the three layers at every 15cm (6in.). Work in lines, or use the pattern of the patchwork as a guide. Trim the ends of the knots to about 15mm (¾in.). They can either be left on top or taken through to the back.

Fig. 16. A reef knot.

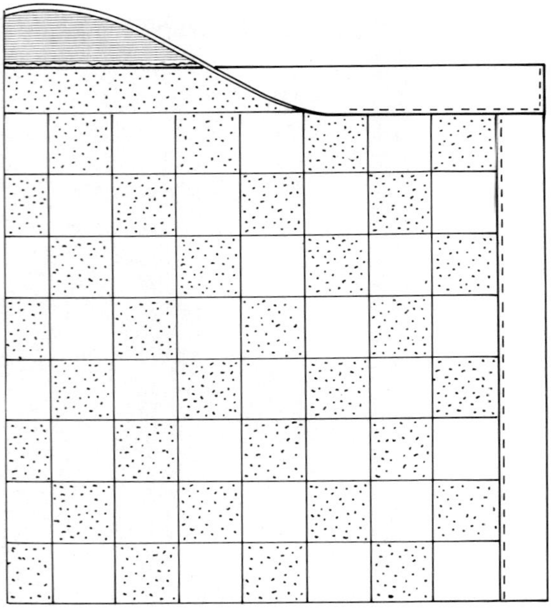

Fig. 17. A self-binding. The corners can be mitred, or left straight as shown above.

FINISHING THE EDGES

A self-binding

This is the quickest and neatest way of finishing the edges around a patchwork. Trim the top fabric and wadding, and measure to check that the patchwork is properly squared up. Bring the backing fabric over to the front, turn a 6mm (¼in.) hem under the raw edge and pin in position. Hand-sew, using a small running stitch around the edge. Hand-stitching is much easier at this stage than machining, as any extra fabric can be gradually eased in. Depending on the width, remember to allow enough wadding so that the edging remains padded with the rest of the quilt. Alternatively the front edges can be turned over to the back.

A separate binding

The advantage of this is that it can be renewed if the edges wear thin. Either use commercial bias binding, 25mm (1in.) wide, or make your own. Attach in the same sequence as the simple straight cut border on page 18. Machine-stitch to the right side first, then turn to the back, pin, and hand-stitch in place.

HANGING A QUILT

Originally patchworks were made for beds, but now they are also used to make colourful wall-hangings. The best way to hang them is by attaching a fabric sleeve along the top edge, extending almost the width of the work. Leave a small gap in the centre in case it is

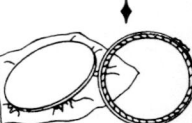

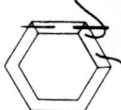

to be hung from a centre point as well as from each end. Make the sleeve about 15cm (6in.) wide, so that it can take a variety of rods or wooden poles. Attach the sleeve with a running-stitch about 3cm (1⅕in.) in from the top edge and sides, so that it does not distort the edges once the pole is in position.

CARE AND CLEANING

Make sure that patchwork is never exposed to strong sunlight, as it will fade and the fibres will be weakened. Keep it regularly brushed to remove dirt and dust. Never store in a plastic bag, which causes mould.

Dry-clean or wash your patchwork, depending on the type of fabric and filling. If it is to be dry-cleaned, choose a specialised cleaners where it will be treated individually.

If all the fabrics and the wadding are washable, then it can be laundered. Wash by hand in the bath, using warm water and a mild detergent — but make certain that the detergent is properly dissolved. Do not rub, just agitate gently, then let it soak for a few minutes. Repeat with fresh water and detergent if the patchwork is heavily soiled. Rinse well, until the water runs clear.

Never twist or wring a quilted patchwork because that will easily break the stitches. Gently squeeze out excess water and give it a short spin if it will fit into a spin-drier.

Try and dry flat on a lawn with a sheet underneath. Avoid direct sunlight.

Never press quilted patchwork with a hot iron, as this will destroy the quilted effect.

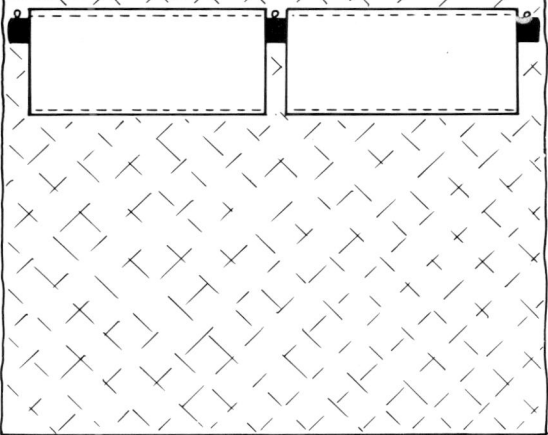

Fig. 18. Sleeve at back of work for hanging rod.

Garden bench cushion (*or window seat, or bedhead*). *'Variable Star'* block. Machine-pieced and hand-quilted. (*Vida James*)

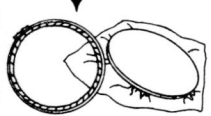

SIZES. Since the metric system offers finer measurement, the sizes in this book have been given in millimetres and centimetres. The imperial equivalent has been given as well, however, to help those less used to working in the metric system.

Back cover:
Shoulder bag. *'Hole in the Barn' block. Machine-pieced and machine-quilted. Both sides of a denim fabric are used, with inset fringed strips of the same fabric. (Pamela Watts)*

Frontispiece:
Throw quilt. *'Indiana Puzzle' or 'Snail's Trail' block. The machine-pieced blocks are alternated with plain squares of fabric. Polyester cotton top and backing, terylene batting. Hand-quilted. (Alison Martin)*

Acknowledgments

Series editor: Kit Pyman

Text and diagrams by Michele Walker.

Text, illustrations, arrangement and typography copyright © Search Press 1983.

Photographs by Search Press Studios

First published in Great Britain in 1983 by Search Press Limited, Wellwood, North Farm Road, Tunbridge Wells, Kent TN2 3DR.

Reprinted 1984, 1985, 1986, 1992

All rights reserved. No model in this book may be reproduced for commercial purposes without the previous written permission of Search Press. No part of this book, text or illustration, may be reproduced or transmitted in any form or by any means by print, photoprint, microfilm, photocopier, or in any way, known or as yet unknown, or stored in a retrieval system, without written permission obtained beforehand from Search Press.

ISBN 0 85532 454 6

Printed in Spain by Elkar, S. Coop.- 48012-Bilbao

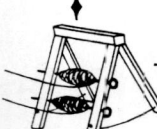